I0488150

A GUIDE TO HOSTING STEM EVENTS

TABLE OF CONTENTS

Introduction

STEM professionals interacting with students at a SEM Link career fair

Science, Technology, Engineering and Mathematics (STEM) is becoming an important topic in our society because we realize that our society is not preparing our students to become a part of the future workforce in a sector that is experiencing job creation and growth. It has become a priority in our educational system, corporate philanthropy and volunteerism, government policy and funding priorities and in the philanthropic sector. In preparing students to become a part of the future STEM workforce, we must engage them in meaningful educational experiences during classroom and out of school time. Classroom engagement is the main responsibility of the department of education (federal and state), school districts (charter, public and private) and the organizations that support them (corporations, foundations, academic institutions etc.). Out of school time engagement can be the responsibility of the schools but it is an opportunity for academic institutions, corporations, community organizations and government agencies to become involved in STEM educational efforts.

One of the ways to provide out of school time STEM educational experiences for youth and their families are STEM events. These events can take place in the evenings, weekends, holiday breaks and summers. STEM events provide schools and organizations with opportunities to engage youth and families in a diversity of ways. STEM events are important because they expand learning beyond the classroom and textbook. The events can be directly connected to what is going on in the classroom, by introducing students to new topics and concepts in STEM by engaging them in hands on or career exploration activities as well as by connecting them with other youth that are interested in STEM.

STEM events can be just for students or they can be for families. They can be an annual event, one-time event or series of events. STEM based events can take place at the school, community organization, college or university or at a local park. The events can be free or fee based. They can be for a specific population or for the general public. The process of planning and hosting STEM events is a long and detailed one that includes many factors and aspects. In this book, we will discuss various aspects of STEM events to help you determine if hosting a STEM event is right for you or your organization. If you or your organization decides that hosting one is right for you, you will learn great tips on how to host a successful event.

Chapter One:
Determining Organizational Capacity for the Event

Alignment with Organization's Mission, Values and Programs

An important part of an organization's sustainability is staying current with trends in order to remain relevant in its industry, receive financial support and/or exercise corporate social responsibility. A huge part of that is developing new programming and/or philanthropic initiatives within the organization. New initiatives and programming are great for an organization because they are the balance between doing the great work that you have always done and staying innovative and relevant to your existing audience while gaining a new audience. However, in this process you must remain true to your organization's mission, values and programming.

In determining if your organization should include STEM events in its programming the first question to answer is "Does it align with your organization's mission?" If your organization's mission isn't connected to STEM or education it may be a stretch for you and may not be a good fit. Even when you feel like it is good to do what is popular right now, staying true to your mission is better for your organization in the long run. Your current stakeholders will be happy that you are staying true to your organization's mission. In addition, you don't have to worry about tarnishing the reputation and brand of your organization or confusing your current and potential target audience by doing something that doesn't align with your mission.

The next question to ask is if hosting a STEM event aligns with your organization's mission. Does it align with your values? Your organization's values guide the perspective and actions of your organization and define the organizational culture. It is important that your organization's values guide your decision making process, instead of trends or funding sources. Does your organization need or want to spend time and energy hosting a STEM event?

The final question to ask is, if hosting a STEM event aligns with your organization's programming. There is always room for an organization to add new programming, but some program activities are a better fit than others. When you think about the programming, you must consider two important factors; your normal program activities and who your organization serves. You must plan an event that aligns with your normal programming activities, so it is a good fit for your organization's programming structure. The event must be one that your target audience, current and potential, would attend if you hosted it.

Professional Expertise/Skill Sets of Your Staff and Volunteers

Once you have determined that hosting a STEM event aligns with your organization's mission, values, and programming, you must consider if your organization can make this event happen. The first step in determining if you can host a successful STEM event that will continue to add value to your brand and programming, is the professional expertise and skill sets of your staff and volunteers. This is important because you need to determine what aspects of planning the event you can do internally and what you will need external support with. It can also determine the type of STEM event your organization hosts.

If your organization's staff and volunteers don't have the professional expertise to host a STEM event, your organization will have to hire or partner with another organization. Prior to getting another individual or organization involved in your event, you have to set the purpose and plan for the event. You must determine what you want to accomplish from the event and what you want it to look like. Before you can bring another person or organization into the event planning process, you must be able to clearly communicate your vision to others. When you are able to clearly communicate your vision and plan, it will allow your organization to use its resources and time wisely.

Organization's Budget and Access to Resources

One of the most important questions to ask before you host an event is how are you going to pay for the event. The first step in determining how you will pay for the event is being sure that you are familiar with your organization's budget. Do you already have the funds in your budget? Be sure that the funds that you think you allocate can be used for an event. If the funds are from grants, be sure that you are using unrestricted grants or grants designated for that purpose. If you have any questions contact the funder before you spend any funds from the particular funding source for the event.

If you don't have the funds for the event, how will you get the funds to pay for the event? Will you set a date for the event in your organization's calendar that will allow you enough time to seek grant funding or event/corporate sponsors? If you are seeking grant funding how will this event fit as a part of a project or program, since most funders don't support events. When soliciting event sponsors, conduct research to determine what organizations will sponsor your event. You can ask organization's that have previously supported your organization to see if they would be willing to support your event. Prior to seeking corporate/event sponsors be sure to create a sponsorship packet that provides information about the sponsorship levels and what you will offer them for their support of your event.

Chapter 2: Types of STEM events

Classes and Workshops

Classes and workshops are events that can engage parents, students or families. Classroom and workshops can be a one-time event (a few hours, half-day, all day) or a series of events over a period of time. Classes and Workshops are based on themes or topics that you want the attendees to walk away from acquiring new knowledge, developing a skill or engaging in hands on activities. Classes and workshops can also include information that students and/or parents need to learn for academic achievement, career exploration or college preparation. Possible ideas for workshops and classes are:

- Bird watching
- Becoming a STEM Major
- Boot Camps
- Kitchen Chemistry
- Robotics

* This photo is from SEM Link's Math and Science Boot Camp; a workshop to equip students with strategies to be college and career ready in STEM

The steps to take prior to hosting a class or workshop are:

1. Determine what you want your attendees to learn from attending your event
2. Determine if what you want them to learn can be taught at a one-time event or a series of events
3. Determine the minimum and maximum number of attendees the class or workshop should have to make it effective and worth the organization's time and energy
4. Determine the type of facility that is ideal as well as a secondary location to host the class or workshop
5. Determine the equipment and/or materials that you will need to host the class or workshop
6. Determine if you organization will develop original content or use content developed by another organization

Campaigns and Contests

Campaigns are a series of activities that take place to produce desired results for various activities within your organization. The participants in campaigns don't necessary receive anything other than the satisfaction of being a part of something bigger than themselves. In this age of technology most campaigns take place via social media. An example of a social media campaign can be to bring awareness to an issue or topic in STEM. A recent social media campaign that took place whose goal was to change the perception of what a STEM professional looks like and does. In this campaign, STEM professionals of African descent where encouraged to post photos of themselves in their workplace on Twitter using the hashtag of the campaign. The participants in this campaign didn't receive anything from their participation in the campaign other than the satisfaction of knowing they highlighted the diversity in STEM.

The non-profit SEM Link, recently hosted a social media campaign, "Dads and Grads" during the month of June. The hashtag #DadsandGrads was used for this campaign. In honor of Father's Day, SEM Link wanted to celebrate the great fathers in this world that are active and engaged in the lives of their children. Since this nonprofit organization's mission is to promote student achievement and career exploration in STEM, it wanted to showcase dad's doing hands on STEM activities with their kids. They took photos that were submitted from families as well as photos of dads with their children at SEM Link events. In honor of graduation season, SEM Link wanted to highlight the high school graduates that were majoring in STEM in the fall. They posted photos of students listing their college and major.

The steps for developing and implementing a campaign are:
1. Determining what is the cause, issue or story you want to highlight.
2. Decide what platform(s) you will use for your campaign, i.e. Twitter, Instagram, Facebook, email etc.
3. Create the theme or name for the campaign
4. Create a hashtag for the campaign
5. Setting a timeline for the campaign (when it will start and end as well as posting schedule)
6. Determining how you want people to participate in the campaign (how the staff and volunteers of your organization will be involved as well as the general public)
7. Announce the campaign to your staff, volunteers and the general public through various channels (it can be email, press release, social media, etc.) prior to the start of the campaign
8. Launch and manage your campaign
9. Recap the highlights of your campaign a few days after it ends.

Contests are events where individuals or teams compete for an honor and/or a prize. Contestants enter a submission (essay, photo, story or video) for a panel of judges to determine the winner(s) of the contest. Contests have a timeframe for accepting submissions, judging the submissions and announcing the winners. All of this should be determined prior to the announcement of the contest. The contest announcement should also include the honor or prize the contest winners will receive. If your organization decides to host a contest these are the steps you should take prior to developing and implementing a contest.

1. Select the theme and name for your contest
2. Determine if the frequency of your contest (one time, monthly, annually)
3. Determine the medium you will accept your entries (essay, photo, story, video)
4. Determine the age group for your contestant
5. Determine contest rules and guidelines
6. Determine how you will accept contest entries
7. Determine a scoring rubric for the contest and select judges
8. Determine the prizes for the contest and how you will secure them
9. Determine how you will market and advertise your contest to get submissions
10. Determine how you will market and advertise your contest to the general public and media outlets
11. Determine how you will notify the contestants of their status in the contest; especially the winners
12. Determine how you will announce the winners? Will you have an awards ceremony? Will you announce via your website and social media outlets?
13. Determine how you will thank everyone involved in the contests (contestants, judges, sponsors, etc.)

Fairs and Festivals

Fairs are events that showcase opportunities, resources, student or organization work. The most common types of fairs are career, health and science fairs. Festivals are events that have a specific focus such as science, engineering, etc. Fairs and festivals can not only for your community organization or school community but you can also invite the general public. At times fairs and festivals have similar themes and/or set ups and can be planned the same way. Be sure to determine planning your fair or festival

1. Determine the focus of your event and what you want to showcase; that will determine if your event will be a fair or festival
2. Determine how many student projects/exhibitors you will have at the event and the selection process for them
3. If you are hosting a STEM or science fair, determine if you are you going to announce winners and/or give prizes for the student work/projects

Math and Science Nights

Math and Science Nights are events that engage families in a STEM activity. These events usually take place evenings and last 1-3 hours and usually include refreshments for attendees. The purpose of Math and Science Nights is to showcase something or provide examples of STEM activities. A school can host a Math and Science Night to showcase student work (coursework, experiments) and introduce parents to the STEM curriculum used by classroom teachers. After-school (out of school time) programs can host a Math and Science Night to showcase to parents and community stakeholders program activities. Community organizations can host a Math and Science Night to provide an activity for its clients and neighbors to engage in. Here are some possible themes for a Math and Science Night

- Back to STEM/School
- Family Literacy Nights
- Chemistry Week Celebrations
- Engineering Design Challenges

The steps to take when planning a Math and Science Night
1. Determine the purpose for hosting your math and science night. Is it more about showcasing student work, providing information to parents or engaging families in STEM activities? It can be a combination of all these things, just be clear about the event's purpose.
2. Set up the structure for the event? How long will the event last, will it be in one location or multiple locations at your site.
3. Determine what materials and/or people you need to make the event a success? Do you need a specific staff person to speak or do you want to bring an outside person at the event?

<u>Chapter 3: Mapping Your Event</u>

Determining Your Target Audience

Before you start to plan an event, you must determine your target audience. Your target audience is the specific group of people that you want to reach with your event. It is formed by people of a certain age group, gender, socioeconomic background and ethnic background. When you select your target audience, you must keep in mind that other groups may be interested in participating in the event. So you must determine if your event will be open to the groups other than your target audience or exclusively for your target audience.

Determining your target audience is one of the most important activities in mapping your event. It guides all the steps that you will take planning, marketing, advertising and hosting your event. Here are a few things to consider when determining the target audience for your event:

- What demographic(s) do you want to reach? This is gender, age group, social economic background, ethnic background, location, etc.
- What are your demographics psychographics (personal characteristics)? What are their values, interests, behaviors, attitudes, lifestyles, etc.
- How will your target audience benefit (what will they get, learn etc.) from attending your event?
- How do you reach your target audience to let them know about your event?
- Will your target audience attend an event hosted by your organization? Do they know about and/or trust your brand?

Event Cash Flow Statement and Pricing

Using an event cash flow statement instead of an event budget takes into consideration both the expenditures and the revenue of an event. An event cash flow statement allows your organization to know its financial resources and obligations at any point during the event planning process. The financial resources that you obtain for the event is the cash inflow and your expenditures are the cash outflow. A cash flow statement should be developed during various stages prior to and after the event. If you are a nonprofit and you have received in-kind goods or service donations, include that in your cash flow statement. This is considered a true revenue source and expenditure. Be sure to make a note in your records that it was in-kind.

Here is an example of revenue and expenditures. This is a general list based on categories. The list your organization creates will be detailed based on the needs of your event.

Possible Revenue Sources	Possible Expenditures
Line item in organization's budget	Event venue costs
Grants	Supplies/equipment
Event sponsors	Food/ entertainment
Ticket sales	Marketing and Advertising

You can find templates for cash flow statements online and/or from your word processing software, but be sure it includes:

1. A list of each revenue source and how much revenue you received from the source
2. A list of each expenditure and how much that expenditure costs your organization

Below is an example of a cash flow statement for a festival about a month prior to the event:

Cash Flow Statement from Science Fiction Film Festival

Revenue

Corporate Sponsors...$3,000.00

Ticket Sales..$1,500.00

Grants.. $2,000.00

Total Revenue **$6,500.00**

Expenditures

Venue Rental...$1,500.00

Event Insurance...$500.00

Festival Speakers and Staff.......................................$1000.00

Audio Visual Rental...$1000.00

Event Marketing and Advertising............................. $1,500.00

Food...$1,000.00

Event Photographer/Videographer...............................$600.00

Film Rights... $400.00

Event Evaluation...$500.00

Total Expenditures...$8,000.00

Total Revenues minus Total Expenditures $6,500- $8,000.00 = (-$1,500.00)

Based on this example cash flow statement, the organization has overspent for the event and needs an additional $1,500 for the event to break even and not lose any money. Based on the revenue sources, the organization can sell more tickets, acquire more sponsors or both to earn the additional revenue needed to host the event.

Event Pricing (Ticket Pricing for Attendees)

It is important that the organization determines what they will charge attendees to participate in the event. This determines if you will be able to host the event and what revenue sources you should secure. Things you need to consider when determining the ticket price for your event include:

- The total cost for hosting your event
- What percentage of the event costs do you want to pass on to the event attendees?
- Does your organization want to cover its cost or make a profit from the event?
- How much do you think your target audience is able and/or be willing to pay to attend the event?
- What are the processing fees or other fees/costs associated with the service you will use to sell tickets

Determining the Event Date, Location and Time

The date, location and time for your event can determine the maximum attendance as well as exposure for your organization.

When selecting the date for events, consider the following things:

- The other programs and projects of your organization; you want to give your organization enough time to devote to planning the event among the other events/projects your organization is responsible for carrying out

- The other major events that your target audience can possibly attend in the area other than yours. When you are in urban areas there is always a possible conflict but you don't want to select a time when the attendance will be low which includes annual events by larger organizations, near holiday breaks/graduation season, etc.
- Ensure that you have adequate time to plan, market and advertise your event to its target audience and the general public

When selecting the location for events consider the following things:

- Is the location accessible to your target location (can they get there easily by car and/or public transportation)?
- Is the parking at the location easy to find and low cost or free for your attendees?
- Does the location have most if not all of the things you need to host the event? For example if you are hosting a science festival, does the space allow you to be able to have a diversity of experiments and provide electricity and water for your exhibitors? If you are hosting a workshop does the facility have access to a LCD projector?
- Does the location have a custodial service or staff that can handle any issues that may arise during the event such as clean-up, safety or security

When determining the time you host your event and/or the duration for your event, consider the following things:

- Determine how much time you need to complete all the activities you want to do at the event
- Determine the best day of the week and time of day for maximum attendance

Chapter 4: Pre-Event Logistics

The event coordination process begins weeks, months and sometimes years prior to the event. In the most successful events, the coordinators give themselves at minimum of 6 months to 9 months prior to the event for planning, especially if it is their first time hosting the event. Starting the planning process for your event early allows you to prepare for the event as well as make any adjustments to any curveballs that may come your way.

Securing Your Location and Working with the Venue

Just like in real estate, location is important. Selecting the right location for your event is a critical component of the event's success. Selecting the location for the event is the first step in the event coordination process after you have selected your tentative date and time. Please keep in mind the following during this phase of event planning:

- Be sure the event rental fees are within your budget
- Be sure to review the contract thoroughly and make sure to account for all potential fees and requirements. (I.e. event insurance, fee for outside food, fee for use of AV equipment etc.)
- Be sure to understand what you are responsible for as far as set up and clean up and what the venue is responsible for.
- Be sure that you pay attention to any clauses in the agreement that may impact the marketing and advertising of your event; especially if you are getting the space as a donation from the venue

Obtaining Resources to Cover Event Expenditures

When you host an event, it will have direct and indirect costs. The indirect costs are the costs associated with the time and energy that your staff spends on the planning the event. Therefore, your organization's staff whether as a part of their regular salary, extra financial compensation, or non-financial compensation such as a flex-time, should be considered in the costs of the event. The direct costs are the costs that your organization only incurs as a result of hosting your event. Your event cash flow statement, which is mentioned in Chapter 3, should include both direct and indirect costs.

Most organizations have budgetary restrictions based on how funds can be used or may not have the funds in the budget at all for hosting events. Therefore, if you want to have an event, you have to find the funding to support the event. The two most common ways of funding an event are event sponsorships and/or ticket sales.

Event sponsorship is when you ask other organizations (academic institutions, corporations, government agencies, professional societies, small and medium sized businesses) to help you with the cost associated with the event. Event sponsorships are not just about getting money for the organization, but building a relationship with other organizations. An organization sponsors your event because of the benefit it provides for them. At times they do it to reach their target market, achieve their community outreach goals or gain publicity. Do not begin to seek corporate sponsors until you have finalized the time, date and location for your event.

Here are a few steps to help in securing sponsors:

1. Do your research on organizations in your area; be sure that you make a list of the organizations that want to reach your target audience for the event and/ or that support a specific focus in the community (i.e. support education, at risk youth, job training etc.)

2. Determine your sponsorship levels and set benefits for each level. Your sponsorship level should have a wide range of levels that allow smaller businesses as well as larger companies to sponsor the event. Be sure that the benefits you offer for sponsorship are something your organization has the capacity to do. In addition, be sure that the benefits increase

with the amount of financial support the organization gives for your event. Some sample benefits are:

- Name mentioned at the event
- Name and/or logo on event materials
- Table at the event
- Name and/or logo on website and/or organization materials
- Name mentioned in event publicity such as press releases and/or social media

3. Develop a system for the event sponsorship process which should include:

- The organizations and contact persons within the organization that you will need to request support
- Who in your organization will be contacting organization to request support and how the organization's that are sponsoring your event should contact.
- Determine how many times you will contact an organization to request support from an organization with no response before moving on to another organization
- A method or technology tool for keeping track of who you contact and when you contacted them
- A system/process for companies to sign up as an event sponsor; whether it be a physical or online form
- A system/process for accepting the event sponsorship fees (i.e. invoicing, online payment, organization/company checks)
- A system/process for keeping track of what organizations signed up as event sponsors and their sponsorship levels
- A system for sending receipts and thanking sponsors

4. Develop a sponsorship packet and proposal letter for soliciting sponsors. Be sure to get a graphic designer to develop a professional document that includes the following:

- Information about your organization
- Information about the event
- Event sponsorship level and benefits
- Photos and/or statistics that will help sell the event
- The procedure for signing up to become an event sponsor
- The contact within your organization that will stay in contact with sponsors

5. Start the event sponsorship solicitation process

- The initial contact via email and phone (Try to send the information via email first then follow up with a phone call)
- Do follow up contacts until you get a yes, no or reached your threshold for number of contacts without a response.
- When you get a yes, be sure to discuss the collection of the sponsorship fees. Ask the following questions:

a) What is the exact amount of financial support they will provide your organization?
b) Will they need an invoice from your organization in order to process payment?
c) What is their method of payment (credit card, check) and the time frame in which your organization should expect payment?
d) Who in their organization should you follow up with if the payment does not arrive within the expected timeframe?

e) When you receive the payment, who do you inform of receipt of the funds? (let your contact person know that you receive payment and within 5 business days send the organization a receipt?

- If the organization says no to your sponsorship, request to add them to your mailing list. There are various reasons an organization says no to a request. Having them on your mailing list keeps the organization abreast of what is going on within your organization and they may choose to support your organization in another manner or at a later date.

6. Acknowledge your sponsors

- Make a list of the organizations that financially supported your event and the amount of their financial support
- Once you've complete the list of sponsors, organize that list based on sponsorship levels.
- Be sure to review your sponsorship packet and acknowledge all the companies in the way that you said that you would do so in your sponsorship packet

Ticket sales are another way to earn revenue for your event. There are four things you need to consider about ticket sales:

1. Pricing– How much you will charge? How much you want to earn from ticket sales? The more you need or want to earn, the higher your ticket prices should be. When determining ticket price, be sure to take into account what your target audience is willing and able to pay to attend your event. Also determine if you will have a different ticket price for advance tickets and tickets sold at the door.

2. Determine the minimum and maximum number of tickets you can sell based on the capacity of the venue and set up of the event.

3. Platform for selling tickets- Will you print tickets to sell or use an online platform such as Eventbrite?

4. Timeframe for selling tickets- Determine the date when ticket sales will begin and end. Also, determine if you will sell tickets at the door.

Event Staffing

In order for an event to run smoothly, your organization will need a certain amount of individuals to handle various tasks for the event. Here are some of the categories that you will need to put staff and volunteers in place for the event. You will also have to determine the number of individuals you need for each category; each will vary based on the size of your event.

- Events set up, clean up and break down- (be sure to review the contract with the venue prior to this process to be clear you know what your organization is responsible for and what the venue staff is responsible for).

  1. Setting up your event is anything that will prepare your event to be ready for its attendees. It includes decorations, signage, any materials/food etc.

  2. Make sure the venue is clean when your attendees arrives, stay cleans throughout the event and when the event is over.

  3. Break down of your event include ensuring the venue is the same way it was when you arrived at the venue and that everything that your organization brought to the venue leaves with your staff or volunteers.

- Check-in and registration- Make sure you have enough people to keep track of the following groups of individuals that will be in attendees at your event.

  1. Event VIP- These are individuals that are important to the main activity of your event. They can include event exhibitors, speakers, entertainment, sponsors, etc.

  2. Pre-registered/Pre-sale attendees and onsite registrants- Be sure to have a process for checking in the pre-registered/pre-sale attendees. Be sure to have multiple copies of your registration list. If you gave pre-registrants the option to pay, onsite be sure to make note of those attendees your registration team should be collecting payment from. For online registration, be sure to have a system for collecting the names and other pertinent information from those who register online as well as the systems for collecting payment.

  3. Media, Community Leaders and Elected Officials- If your event happens to have these individuals you want to make sure at some point your acknowledge your community leaders and elected officials during the event. For the media, you want to make sure they have all the information they need as well as access to take good pictures and/or video to cover your event in their publication and/or live stream the event.

  4. Volunteers- If your event has volunteers that will be assisting with event be sure to have a place where they will check in that includes the names and assignment of each volunteer. Always have assignments prepared in advance for each volunteer. You can make adjustments to their assignment when they arrive if necessary.

- Main Event/ Activity- Whether the individuals are your staff, volunteers or invited guests be sure that you have all the individuals you need to host the main activity for your event.

Event Advertising and Marketing

Event marketing and advertising serves three major purposes; getting your target audience to the event, informing the general public about your event, and bringing attention and awareness to the work of your organization. Use multiple channels, both traditional and social media, as well as create marketing materials for your event. Here are some tools to use in your event marketing and advertising toolbox:

1. Event Flyer- The flyer is the first thing that you should create for your event after you've finalized the date, time, location, and ticket price of your event. The flyer should be attention grabbing and include pertinent information about your event (location, date, time, how to register/purchase tickets and organization contact information). The flyer should have a digital version that you can post online and/or send to your network via text as well as a printable version.

2. Press Release- A press release is a written communication directed to the media announcing your event. You can issue a press release by emailing it to your organizations media list, posting it online platforms such as www.prlog.org and/or positing it on your website. The press release should include pertinent information about your event, a quote from organization leadership and/or key stakeholders such as partners or sponsors, and short description of your organization.

3. Public Service Announcement (PSA) - PSA's are short messages produced for media outlets to help promote your event. They can be a written statement, audio recording or video. The written statements are usually posted on the media outlets community calendar or on-air personalities use the PSA's to make on air announcements. Audio and video recording can be posted on the media outlets website, during commercial breaks or the designated times that media outlets air PSA's.

4. Street Teams- These individuals from your organization you may have visit events and/or places where your target audience will be present to hand out flyers and/or announce your event.
5. Social Media Advertising- Your organization can use social media to advertise your event by creating an event on Facebook, a video on YouTube and creating specific content for each of your social media platforms. Your organization can also purchase ads on social media platforms to promote your event.

Chapter 5: Event Day Logistics

The day of your event is here and you want to make sure that all your hard work, time and energy has prepared you to make your event a success. As an event organizer, there is always something that may not go as you planned or envisioned, but the key is to not let anything happen that damages your brand. Here are things that you need to do in order to ensure that your event is organized and successful.

1. Event staff/volunteer scheduling- Be sure that you have adequate event staff/volunteers whose schedule is staggered throughout the event. This will ensure that the work is spread around during the event as well as that you have adequate coverage to handle the event as scheduled and any "emergencies" that take place during the vent.

2. Have your event ready and set up on time for event VIP's and attendees- Your event has two groups of people that your organization must be prepared for and ready to receive when they arrive; event VIPs and general attendees. This may require your staff to arrive a few hours prior to the start of your event to be prepared for both groups. Your staff will have to stagger your set up for each group because you never know how long set up will take.

- VIP set up- prior to the arrival of your VIP's general signage, information about where the VIP's will conduct the activity you brought them in to support and any materials or equipment. It may also be good to have a dedicated person throughout the event that can be a point person for your VIP
- General attendees- Be sure that you have the registration table set up and ready for your event. You should have your registration table and event set up ready, expecting that there will be attendances that will arrive as early as 30 minutes prior to the start of your event.

3. Be respectful of the time of your attendees by starting and ending your event on time. If there is any unforeseen circumstances that cause your event to start late, be sure to communicate that to attendees. If you start late and are able to remove or reduce the time of an activity in the event do so in order to end on time. If you are unable to remove or reduce the time of an activity, create and communicate a new schedule to the attendees that keeps the event within the same allotted time scheduled for the event.

5. Keep an accurate count of and collect data (name, demographic information and contact information) about everyone that attends your event. (This is where a good registration/check in process is important). You should count your volunteers, event VIP's and attendees (pre-registered/pre-sale and onsite). Keeping an accurate count and collecting data will allow you to do the following things:

- Have event data to report to your key stakeholders (sponsors, boards) via emails, reports, your website and social media outlets.

- Build and maintain a database of attendees and volunteers that you can use to stay in regular communication with them for support of your organization in various ways (future attendance at events, volunteering or donating to the organization)

- Measure the success and/or identify areas of improvement for your event to determine if you met your goals and objectives for hosting the event as well as to see if you were able to reach your target audience or expand your reach by hosting the event.

5. Be sure to have an event photographer/videographer as well as designated volunteers and staff taking photos and videos of during the event. Also consider live streaming and/or posting on social media during your event; creating an event hashtag will help the event trend on social media. You can ask your attendees to post as well using the event hashtag.

6. Create an evaluation survey to get feedback from attendees, volunteers, and sponsors. You can either hire an evaluation consultant or create a short survey via platforms such as Google Drive, Survey Monkey or Zoomerang. Use that data to create evaluation reports which you can use internally to plan for the next event and give to key stakeholders such as sponsors and funders. At times quotes from surveys can be used as testimonials on your website or reports.

Chapter 6: Post Event Logistics

Congratulations! Your event is over, but before you rest and relax or move on to the next project be sure to do the following to properly close out your event.

1. Pay all of your bills

    - Most of your bills/expenditures will be due prior to the event, but just in case do a final check to make sure that everyone is paid. If you have any issues paying everyone communicate with that party your expected date of payment.

2. Say thank you

    - Send personal thank you notes and/or emails to your sponsors, VIP's and volunteers

    - Send thank you emails to your attendees as well as thank you social media posts

    - Send thank you correspondence to the staff members within your organization that were an integral part of the event planning and helped out the day of the event.

3. Share the story of your event
    - Share event data, pictures and email lists with event sponsors. This is important because they provided the financial support to host the event. You can do this via email and/or U.S. mail.

    - Share event data and pictures with event volunteers and attendees via email.

- Share event data and pictures via your newsletter, via an email to your email list as well as social media outlets

- Share event data and pictures with the media, elected officials and community leaders via a post-event press release and letters via email or U.S. mail.

STEM Event Planning Brainstorming Exercise

This exercise will help you brainstorm and determine if a STEM event is a right fit for your organization prior to you starting the event planning process in this book.

1. Why does your organization want to host a STEM event?

2. If the STEM event is a new initiative or program activity does it align with your current programming goals?

3. Does your organization have funds allocated within its budget to host a STEM event? If yes, list the funding sources and/or budget line items you can use for the event? If not, how do you plan to get the funds?

4. What type of STEM event does your organization want to host? Why did you select this type of event?

5. What does success with this event look like to your organization?

Appendix

- [Sample Project/Event To Do List](#) from Microsoft Office
- [How to Write A Press Release](#) from prlog.org
- [Tips for Writing A Public Service Annoucement (PSA)](#) from essortment.com
- Sample for to [Submit an Event to a Media Outlet's Community Calendar](#)

About the Author

A native of Miami, Florida and an alumnus of Florida A & M University, Ms. Tokiwa T. Smith is a social entrepreneur and science, technology, engineering and mathematics (STEM) educator with over 10 years' experience working in education and philanthropy. She has worked for organizations such as Atlanta Public Schools, Georgia State University and Spelman College. Ms. Smith is Founder and Executive Director of Science, Engineering and Mathematics Link Inc. (SEM Link), a national non-profit organization that promotes student achievement and career exploration in math and science for K-12 students by connecting them to the STEM community. SEM Link's two core programs, *Experimental Design Program* and *Math and Science Career Academy*, enhance the STEM educational experience for K-12 students by providing them with opportunities to engage in hands-on STEM activities, explore STEM careers and learn about real-world applications of STEM. Since its inception in 2005 it has served thousands of youth in Atlanta, DMV (DC, Maryland and Virginia) and the San Francisco Bay areas.

Ms. Smith is also the Chief Executive Officer and Principal Owner of Kemet Educational Services, a math and science educational consulting firm that provides supports to community organizations, educational programs, parent groups and schools. She is the San Francisco/Oakland contributor for BlackGivesBack, a blog that has over 50,000 readers nationally that focuses on African Americans in philanthropy. She also has her own blog The Science Socialite , where she writes about her journey as a social entrepreneur and STEM educator. Ms. Smith conducts workshops on various STEM education topics and serves on the advisory board of several STEM educational programs. Ms. Smith's work has been featured in several media outlets. In 2013 she was named as one **Ebony Magazine's 10 Black Twitter Tweeps to Watch!** and in 2014, she was featured on **NPR's Tell Me More** *Women Digital Thinkers Tweet for A Day* She currently resides in Oakland, CA.